THE BLUE PETER BOOK OF LIMERICKS

THE BLUE PETER BOOK OF LIMERICKS

Edited by Biddy Baxter and
Rosemary Gill

with illustrations by
Peter Firmin
and Edward Lear

A Piccolo Book

PAN BOOKS LTD : LONDON
in association with the
BRITISH BROADCASTING CORPORATION

First published 1972 by Pan Books Ltd,
33 Tothill Street, London, SW1,
in association with the British Broadcasting Corporation,
35 Marylebone High Street, London, W1.

ISBN 0 330 02959 2

Printed and Bound in England by
Hazell Watson & Viney Ltd,
Aylesbury, Bucks

This book is dedicated to
the 8,229 'Blue Peter' viewers
who entered our Limerick Competition

INTRODUCTION

There was a young fellow called Pete,
Who was always most tidy and neat.
When he stood on his head
Both Val and John said,
'Oh, look at his nice little feet!'

Mark Stainforth
Age: 10

That was one of the eight thousand two hundred and
twenty-nine entries for our 'Blue Peter' Limerick Competition. This colossal number of entries just goes to show how
popular verse writing is – especially when it's funny. Because
that's one of the best things about limericks, they nearly
always give you a giggle.

There was a young fellow called Green,
Whose musical sense was not keen;
He said: 'It's most odd,
But I cannot tell God
Save the Weasel from *Pop Goes the Queen*!'

That's not a new limerick, it's one that's been going around for ages. But we thought 'Blue Peter' viewers were so good at inventing things they'd be bound to come up with something just as funny, so we thought we'd have a Competition.

A good limerick is not an easy thing to write. When you read them, you might think they're simple to invent, but they're not because there are rules you have to stick to. Limericks always have five lines and they're always nonsensical. The secret is to have a story in your limerick, to get a good couple of rhymes and always to have a funny last line.

It doesn't necessarily matter if you can't get the lines to scan or be an equal length as you can see from this one:

There was a young man of Japan
Who wrote verse that never would scan.
When they said 'But the thing
Doesn't go with a swing,'
He said, 'Yes but I always like to get
as many words into the last
line as I possibly can.'

Before we started our Competition we found out quite a lot about limericks, and the thing that surprised us most of all was that they're certainly not a modern invention. In fact, they're so old nobody's quite sure how they started, but something most people agree about is that they began in Ireland. As as long ago as the year AD 800, Irishmen were writing verses in this rather peculiar way. They didn't have jokes in them in those days but they all had five lines and they all went with a swing when you said them. So much so, that scholars call the rhythm of the verses the 'swinging metre'.

Nobody knows for sure why a limerick is called a limerick, but it's also the name of one of the most famous towns in Ireland. In the middle of the eighteenth century the landlord of a tavern in Mungret Street, Limerick City, John 'The Gay' O'Tuomy wrote splendid limericks – like this for example:

I sell the best brandy and sherry,
To make my good customers merry,
But at times their finances,
Run short, as it chances,
And then I feel very sad, very.

John O'Tuomy had a friend who replied to this. He was called Andrew Magrath, and he said:

O, Tuomy! you boast yourself handy,
At selling good ale and bright brandy,
But the fact is your liquor,
Makes everyone sicker,
I tell you that, I, your friend Andy.

As the years passed, limericks spread to this country. In 1820 a set was written called *Anecdotes and Adventures of Fifteen Young Ladies*; then another one came out called *The History of Sixteen Wonderful Old Women*. There were sixteen separate limericks, each one about a different old woman, and they certainly were a very peculiar lot!

There was an old woman of Gosport,
And she was one of the cross sort.
When she dressed for the Ball,
Her wig was too small,
Which enrag'd this old woman of Gosport.

There was an old woman named Towl,
Who went out to sea with her owl.
But the owl was seasick,
And scream'd for Physic,
Which sadly annoyed Mistress Towl.

There dwelt an old woman at Exeter,
When visitors came it sore vexed her.
So for fear they would eat
She lock'd up all the meat,
This stingy old woman at Exeter.

One of the first complete books of limericks to be published was called *A Book of Nonsense*. It was published in 1846 and the author was Edward Lear. He was actually a painter, so it seems strange he came to write a nonsense book, but it all started when he was working in the country mansion of the Earl of Derby. Edward Lear had been asked to do some coloured paintings of the Earl's collection of parrots. As well as parrots, the Earl had a lot of grandchildren, and Edward Lear somehow had to keep them amused as well. So he started writing his limericks, and to go with each one, he drew a little sketch.

There was an Old Man of the Coast,
Who placidly sat on a post;
But when it was cold
He relinquished his hold
And called for some hot buttered toast.

There was an Old Lady whose folly
Induced her to sit on some holly,
Whereon by a thorn,
Her dress being torn,
She quickly became melancholy.

There was an Old Man who said: 'How
Shall I flee from this horrible cow?
I will sit on this stile,
And continue to smile,
Which may soften the heart of that Cow.'

There was an Old Man who supposed
That the street door was partially closed;
But some very large rats
Ate his coat and his hats,
While that futile Old Gentleman dozed.

There was an Old Man of the West,
Who never could get any rest;
So they set him to spin
On his nose and his chin,
Which cured that Old Man of the West.

There was an Old Person of Ewell,
Who chiefly subsisted on gruel;
But to make it more nice
He inserted some mice,
Which refreshed that Old Person of Ewell.

There was an Old Man, who when little
Fell casually into a Kettle;
But, growing too stout,
He could never get out,
So he passed all his life in that Kettle.

The Earl of Derby's grandchildren thought these were
great fun, and, when the *A Book of Nonsense* was published,
so did everyone else. Limerick writing became very popular,
and many great authors turned their hand to them. W. S.
Gilbert, the writer of the famous Gilbert and Sullivan
operas, even wrote one that *didn't* rhyme:

There was an old man of St Bees,
Who was stung in the arm by a wasp.
When asked, 'Does it hurt?'
He replied, 'No it doesn't,
I'm so glad it wasn't a hornet.'

There's also a well-known limerick full of deliberate spell-
ing mistakes:

The Lifeboat that's kept at Torquay,
Is intended to float in the suay.
The crew and coxswain,
Are sturdy as oxswain,
And as smart and as brave as can be.

But it was in 1907 that the craze for limericks really caught on.

Each week two famous London magazines ran competitions for the best limericks and hundreds of thousands of people used to enter.

It was just like the football pools today. The entrance fee for the competition was sixpence, and everybody used to buy sixpenny postal orders to send with their entries.

In 1907 the sale of sixpenny postal orders rocketed from one hundred thousand to over one and a quarter million a month!

Since then people have never stopped writing limericks. There are even been limerick competitions set by disc jockeys on Radio One. And like nursery rhymes in the olden days, when something new or unusual happens in the world, someone, somewhere, will come up with a limerick about it.

At the Count Down a bold Astronaut
Thought that Mission Control had said 'Nought.'
But that hero's Zero
Was just a mis-hear, so
He orbited more than he ought!

An old Jobbing Gardner called Tod,
Found decimal currency odd.
As he thumbed through his purse
He let out a curse;
'They're as like as 2p in a pod!'

An elephant born in Tibet,
One day in its cage wouldn't get.
So its keeper stood near–
Stuck a hose in its ear,
And invented the first Jumbo Jet.

A careless old cook from Salt Ash,
In her second-hand car had a crash.
She drove straight through a wall,
House, garden and all,
And ended up Bangers and Mash.

   Thursday, September 23rd, 1971, was the day we announced our Competition and two days later the first entries arrived. By the closing date Monday, October 4th, 1971, you could hardly get inside the 'Blue Peter' office for the stacks of mail bags, paper and envelopes, and by then we were all practically thinking in rhyme. An enormous number of entries were about *us*, and every conceivable rhyme seemed to have been thought of for our surnames of Noakes, Purves and Singleton. Amongst other things John was chopping down Oaks, chatting to Blokes, telling Jokes, visiting his Folks, driving Mini-Mokes – and he even had a pet frog called Croaks:

There was a young fellow called Noakes,
Who was famous for terrible jokes.
But when it was known
That the jokes weren't his own,
He was run out of town as a hoax.

Peter was given a good Tennis Service and tended to feel Nervous:

A cautious young fellow called Purves,
Said 'No, of course I'm not nervous.
It's just that I like
To go on a bike.
A bus could end up topsy-turves.'

Valerie's name proved most difficult of all. The most common rhymes were Gallery and Salary:

A lovely young lady named Valerie,
Charms us all, from the pit to the gallery.
With her feminine grace,
And her lovable face,
Dammit! I'd double her salary.

But not many people managed to dream up a rhyme for Singleton!

The eight thousand two hundred and twenty-nine entries came from all over Britain, from people of all ages, ranging from a boy of four and a half to an eighty-two-year-old nun.

The standard was really very high, and it was an exceedingly difficult job choosing the winners.

One problem was that lots of people made up very similar

limericks, using the same rhymes. There were literally hundreds about trips to the moon and hundreds more about rockets and pockets, and Ealing and ceilings. There were even more about young men from Peru, and a great many about young ladies from Bombay.

Some people just couldn't think of an idea of their own so they decided that instead they'd send us their favourite limerick. They weren't eligible for the Competition because the verses had been going around for ages, but like all good jokes they made us laugh – even though we had heard them before:

There was a young lady of Lynn,
Who was so uncommonly thin,
That when she essayed
To drink lemonade,
She slipped through the straw and fell in.

There was an old man of Peru,
Who dreamt he was eating his shoe.
He awoke in the night
In a terrible fright,
And found it was perfectly true!

There was a young lady from Ryde
Who ate a green apple and died;
The apple fermented
Inside the lamented,
And made cider inside her inside.

There was an old man fron Nantucket,
Who kept all his cash in a bucket.
His daughter, named Nan,
Ran away with a man,
And as for the bucket, Nan tucket.

There was a young man of Bengal
Who went to a fancy dress ball;
He thought he would risk it
And go as a biscuit,
But a dog ate him up in the hall.

But out of all the thousands of entries that were completely original we eventually made our choice. To be fair, we divided the Competition into three age groups. The sevens and under, the eights, nines and tens and the elevens and over.

Because the limericks were so good it was quite impossible to pick out first, second and third prizewinners in each section, so we decided to award eight top prizes in each age group including three first prizes, and there were hundreds of awards for runners-up as well. But perhaps the most exciting news of all was that because the standard of 'Blue Peter' viewers' limerick writing was so high, we were able to put the best ones into a book.

We thoroughly enjoyed reading *all* the entries, whether or not they ended up winning prizes, but it's good to know that because of this book, the top limericks will be in print for people to read for ever and ever – and here they are!

Valerie Singleton.   John Noakes.

Peter Purves.

TOP PRIZEWINNERS

A hungry old goat named Heather,
Was tied up with an old bit of leather.
In a minute or two
She had chewed it right through,
And that was the end of her tether.

> Celia McMaster
> Age: 12

There was a sweet pussy called Jason,
Whose bed was a washing-up basin.
And he said 'It's a fine
Little place to recline,
And to spend the rest of my days in.'

> Fiona Roberts
> Age: $12\frac{1}{2}$

There was an old lady of Venice,
She was such a silly old menace.
Her surname was Brown,
She walked upside down,
And her son and her daughter played tennis.

Catherine Mary Fardell
Age: 7

22

There once was a cat called Pat,
Who grew most incredibly fat.
She sat on the floor
And ate more and more,
And that was the end of that.

Josephine Humble
Age: $7\frac{3}{4}$

23

I really think John's had enough!
Wee Shep is most terribly rough!
He nips poor John's ears
Till he's nearly in tears.
I'd cover them up with a muff!

Andrew Pender
Age: 8

There once was a show called 'Blue Peter',
Whose compères tried out a three-seater.
Val fell in a hole,
John climbed up a pole,
Then up came a wind and blew Peter.

Stephen Hollinghurst
Age: $8\frac{1}{2}$

There was a great train called 'Blue Peter',
And the team of that name went to meet her,
They drew such a crowd
And they felt very proud,
To be naming that steam train 'Blue Peter'.

Anne Sylvester
Age: 9

There was a young lady from Reading,
Who was dying to go to a wedding.
So she bought a big hat,
With a veil and all that,
But she couldn't see where she was heading.

Kathryn Wright
Age: 9

25

There was a young man called Pete Purves,
Who worked in the BBC Service,
He began with a splash,
And once had a crash,
But jumping from heights makes him nervous.

Hilary Pearce
Age: 7

There was a young lady from Bristol,
Who said, 'It's clear as crystal,
"Blue Peter's" the best,
Shoot down all the rest,'
Said this girl with a pistol from Bristol.

Jonathan Wilkins
Age: 11

There was a young lady called Val,
Who said to John Noakes, 'Be a pal,
I've run out of money,
It's really not funny,
And my taxi's got stuck in the Mall.'

Lucinda McDonald
Age: 7

There was a composer called Strauss.
Who lived with a rat and a mouse.
Said Johann one day,
'I am glad they can stay,'
So they all did a waltz round the house.

Patrick Hayward
Age: 6

A spiny young hedgehog called Norman,
Applied for a job as a doorman,
When they saw his fierce snout,
And the way it stuck out,
They decided to call for a lawman.

Laura Empson
Age: 8

There was once a brown dog called Spot,
Who tied up his tail with a knot,
To remember his bone,
Which he'd left back at home,
When he sometimes went out for a trot.

Rebecca Telford
Age: 7

29

My brother and I are called twins
They say we're alike as two pins.
But as he's four foot three,
A bit taller than me,
In races he always just wins.

David Harrison
Age: 9

There was a young lady of Brussels,
Who happened to be fond of mussels.
What she liked was the shells,
Not the mussels themselves,
So her stomach gave off little rustles.

Sally Deith
Age: 9

There was a young man called Pete,
Whose hair hung down to his feet.
Said Val to John,
'It's getting too long,
We can't let him out on the street.'

Karen Fisher
Age: 10

There was a young hamster named Nelly,
Whose whiskers were sticky and smelly,
This was not, if you please,
Some strange new disease,
But a 'strordinary liking for jelly!

Maureen (Min) Lacey
Age: 11

There was a young man from the States,
Came to Britain with some of his mates.
But their car was too wide
For our countryside,
So they left with half of our gates.

Martin Mobberley
Age: 13

There was a young pup from 'Blue Peter',
Who became a remarkable eater.
He ate John and Pete,
Then had Val, as a treat.
Now he's slimming to make himself neater.

John Hossack
Age: 13

There once was a fellow called Cain,
Who, like Noakes, had jokes on the brain.
When his best friend called Harris,
Swam a river in Paris,
Cain shouted 'You must be in-Seine.'

Peter Hennig
Age: 13

There was a young man of Arbroath,
Who kept for a pet a large sloth,
He said, 'It's quite nice,
But it doesn't like mice,
So I buy fish and chips for us both.'

Deborah Westover
Age: 11

There was an old lady from Beddy,
Who went for a walk with a teddy.
And when they came back
The teddy was fat,
Because he had eaten the lady.

Robert Whitaker
Age: 6

There once was a man with a slipper,
Who slashed at a very fat Kipper,
He chopped it in two
And said 'This will do,
To eat for my lunch and my sipper.'

Andrew Fisher
Age: 6

RUNNERS-UP

There was a young fellow called Peter,
Whose height was only one metre,
When asked why this was,
He said 'it's because,
It makes me look very much neater.'

Judith Franklin
Age: $8\frac{1}{2}$

There once was a fellow called Dan,
With a waist of remarkable span,
He exclaimed 'How it pinches
Around all my inches,
I must lose 40 stone if I can.'

James Walmsley
Age: 10

There is a young boxer named Walter,
Who comes from the island of Malta.
One day in the ring,
He stepped on a spring,
And bounced all the way to Gibraltar.

David McDermott
Age: 13

I had a young hamster called Pete,
Who liked to eat very tough meat,
He went out just now,
And swallowed a cow,
And now he's just dead on his feet.

Margaret Hamilton
Age: 9

There was a young man called John Noakes,
Who told a great many jokes.
He drove Val up the wall,
But she laughed at them all,
And then toddled off home to her folks.

Tracy Vaughan-Hodkinson
Age: 7

There was a young laddie called Tony,
Who ate plates of fried macaroni,
He got very fat,
But he didn't mind that,
'Cos he bounced when he fell off his pony.

Belinda Kellett
Age: 8

39

There was a young girl called Pam,
Who turned up her nose at some ham,
But when offered some cheese,
She would say 'Oh yes please,
Though I'm slimming as much as I can.'

Katherine Saunders
Age: 10

My brother's name is Keith,
He hates to clean his teeth,
His dirty face
Is a real disgrace,
But he's lovely underneath.

Brian Bell
Age: 5

There was a young man from Athlone,
Who went in a public phone.
He pressed button 'B',
And much to his glee,
He got tuppence that wasn't his own.

Christine Guidetti
Age: 15

There was a young fella called Clouse,
Who was scared of a tiny wee mouse,
He saw one called Hicks,
Who ran straight up his knicks,
And he shrieked and fled into the house.

Rhona McKinnon
Age: 8

Three people called Val, John and Pete
Made themselves some chocolate to eat.
When a man called Mickey
Asked if it was sticky,
Val replied 'Yes it is, in the heat.'

Daniel Miles
Age: 6

There once was a programme – 'Blue Peter' –
Asked for Limericks with plenty of metre,
They arrived host by host,
Inundating the post,
And buried poor John, Val and Peter.

Andrew Jones
Age: 9

There was an old lady from Rye,
Who was terribly terribly shy.
When a person came near,
She would cower with fear,
Or hide in a corner and cry.

Rosamund Hoskins
Age: 11

There was a young butcher from York,
Whose face was as round as a cork,
The reason he said,
Was the air in his head,
Which he'd swallowed while taking a walk.

Julia Wright
Age: 9

A certain young fellow called Peter,
Went out to buy oil for his heater,
He asked for a quart,
But the man said 'You ought
To know now that it's bought by the litre.'

Claire Allen
Age: 11

There was a millionaire,
Who ate up a yellow green pear,
He said 'It's not nice,
It's been gnawed by the mice,
But I'll eat it because I don't care.'

James Tarry
Age: $5\frac{3}{4}$

There was a young fellow called John,
Who jumped with a parachute on,
He murmured 'I hope,
When I pull on this rope,
I won't find the chute has gone wrong.'

James Walmsley
Age: 10

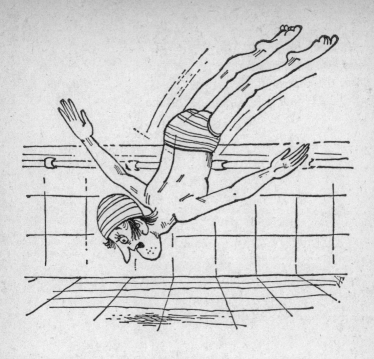

There was a young man called Jim,
Who thought he would go for a swim,
He jumped in the pool,
And felt such a fool,
Because there was no water in.

Susan Leigh
Age: 8

There was a headmaster called Skinner,
At games he was always a winner,
He won games of chess,
And went to Loch Ness,
Then had the monster for dinner.

Fergus Cross
Age: 9

There once was a tortoise called Speedy,
Whose eye was ever so beady,
His mate was called Kate,
Green lettuce they ate,
And lived in a run that was weedy.

Christopher R. Randell
Age: $7\frac{1}{2}$

We have a cousin called Neil,
Who went up on the big Ferris Wheel,
But halfway around,
He looked down at the ground,
And it cost him a 50 pence meal.

Johnnie McCann
Age: 9

There was a young fellow called Guy,
Who desperately wished he could fly,
He made himself wings,
Out of paper and things,
And very soon fell from the sky.

Guy Philipps
Age: 10

There was a young fellow named Teddy,
Who drank beer, and became quite unsteady,
He wobbled away,
And was missing all day,
But came back when his supper was ready.

Gareth Yates
Age: 7½

A policeman when out on his beat,
Was approached by a lady so sweet,
Then he lifted his arm,
Said 'You'll come to no harm,'
And a lorry ran over her feet.

Susan Porter
Age: 8

There was a young boy called Danny,
Who wanted to visit his nanny,
He got on the bus,
Without any fuss,
But he never had any money.

Daniel Paul Cundy
Age: 4¾

There was a young man with a fox,
Which slept in a cardboard box,
It went into town,
To buy a nightgown,
And returned with some red and white socks.

Jeremy Chantrill
Age: 10

There was once a tailor called Pinn,
Who only made suits for the thin,
To keep out the fat,
He stood on the mat,
And only let thin ones come in.

Natasha Willis
Age: 8

There was an old lady from Dorset,
Who couldn't do up her corset.
No matter how hard,
Eased with butter and lard,
She found the only way was to force it!

Celia Bishop
Age: 11

A certain young goalie called Finn,
Lost count of the shots he let in,
When his skipper bawled 'that's eight,'
He replied quite sedate,
'Then we only need nine goals to win.'

Mark Rothery
Age: 8

There was a young man from Crail
Who decided to ride on a whale,
When he got on its back,
It gave him a crack,
With the flap on the end of its tail.

S. Bowman
Age: 10

There was an old, old man,
Who found a big, big pan,
When he had it,
He found a rabbit,
And made some rabbit jam.

Hugh David Muschamp
Age: 5

There once was a big hairy yeti,
Whose favourite food was spaghetti,
He minced it all day,
'Cos he liked it that way,
And his friend said it looked like confetti.

Jonathan Way
Age: 7

There was a young man from Spain,
Who loved to swim in the rain.
He swam in the gutter,
Then started to splutter,
And fell out of sight down a drain.

Alison Jones
Age: 12

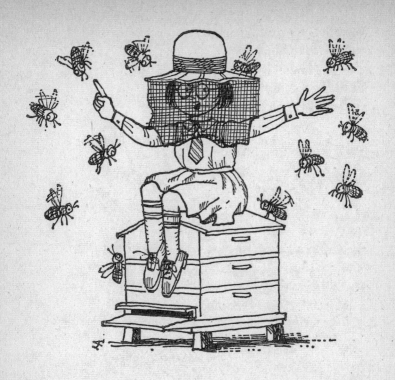

There was a young lady from Blythe,
Who foolishly sat on a hive,
As the bees buzzed around,
With a terrible sound,
She said, 'Oh why don't you bee-hive?'

Gillian Hunt
Age: 9

53

My favourite programme's 'Blue Peter',
There's Val who could not be sweeter,
There's also John Noakes,
With his beautiful jokes,
And a nice young fellow called Peter.

Nicola Stonehouse
Age: 6½

There was a young fellow called Noakes,
Who chopped down some very large oaks.
He was so very good,
That he cleared all the wood,
That amazing young fellow called Noakes.

Martin Phillips
Age: 7

There once was a pussy called Jason,
Who off to the larder did hasten,
He licked up a dish
Of very fine fish,
And lapped up the cream in a basin.

Susannah Walmsley
Age: 7

There was an old man of Beirut,
Who possessed a peculiar coot,
Before going to bed,
It would stand on its head,
And play *Old King Cole* on the flute.

Jonathan Franklin
Age: 10

There was a young lady called Janet,
With a figure the shape of this planet.
When discussing the mile,
She thought for a while,
Then stood up, quickly, and ran it.

Krystyna Januszczyk
Age: 14

There was an old person from Pinner,
Who could not stop eating his dinner,
He grew so fat,
After eating his cat,
That funny old man from Pinner.

Andrew Baird
Age: 6

There was an old stoker from Lee,
So dirty and grimy was he,
That his mates washed him clean,
In the ocean so green,
And that's how we got the Black Sea.

John Tuckwell
Age: 11

There was a poor moggie from Hyde,
Who heard that next door's dog had died.
He went through the gate,
Met a terrible fate,
'Cos the cat that had told him had lied!

Richard Booth
Age: 11

There once was a girl on 'Blue Peter',
Whose steeds were well known to defeat 'er,
She fell off a horse,
As a matter of course,
While a camel could always unseat 'er.

Rachel Walmsley
Age: 12

There was an old lady from Hull,
Who found life terribly dull,
She flew to the moon,
But although she went soon,
She found it was already full.

Rose Pollock
Age: 6

Our Val went down from 'Blue Peter',
To Oxford to fly a two seater.
Though she learnt in a day.
Let us hope BEA
Have the pilots to do the job neater.

Carolyn Porter
Age: 10

All the boys from Methill
Made fun of a girl named Ethel.
Then with a thud,
They landed in mud,
They didn't know Ethel could wrethle.

Michael Jess
Age: 12

59

Susan's the name of my dolly,
I was going to call her Polly,
Or Rachel or Rosy,
Or Penny or Posy,
Or Clara or Sara or Holly.

Sandra Hodgkiss
Age: 7

A man who once took penicillin,
Remarked that it was very fillin',
'But it would be easier,' he said,
'To eat the mould off my bread,
But I'm afraid I'm not very willin'.'

Rosemarie Walter
Age: 15

There was a young man called Terry,
Whose nose was as red as a berry.
His hair was so long,
That it reached to Hong Kong,
And to comb it he went by the ferry.

Angela Cox
Age: 11

My father, he sat on a chair,
For sitting, he has quite a flair.
But the chair it went crack,
He fell flat on his back.
I'd have laughed, but I just didn't dare.

Thérèse Saward
Age: 13

61

There was a young lady who said,
Now remember I want a good spread,
With puppy dogs tails,
And brown roasted snails,
She ended up sick in her bed.

Susan Jones
Age: 10

Said a zoo man, 'I've nursed a sick goat,
I've sat up all night with a stoat.
I've bandaged a flea,
But what worries me
Is a giraffe with a flippin' sore throat.'

Pauline Sword
Age: 11

There was a young fellow called Fred,
Had an elephant sit on his head.
Where the elephant sat,
Fred's head grew quite flat,
But Fred didn't care, he was dead!

Audrey Freeland
Age: 12

A show jumper started his round,
And took the first jump with a bound.
He drove his poor horse
Through the big jump of gorse,
And ended up flat on the ground.

Katie Stevens
Age: 12

In rehearsing our play, *Robin Hood*,
Nobody did as they should,
The travellers died,
The merry men cried,
And only the teachers were good.

Hilary Jane Morris
Age: 11

Adam was ready for bed,
When a tooth fell out of his head.
Hip hip hooray,
That's made my day.
I'll have 5np instead.

Adam Fitch
Age: 7

There was a young lady of Stroud,
Who started to sing very loud,
When neighbours heard her,
They said they preferred her,
To sing far away on a cloud.

Dawn Broadbent
Age: 10

There was an old lady of Ayr,
Who kept a pet mouse in her hair,
She fed it on cheese,
And made it say 'please',
Before she would give it its share.

Brian Smyth
Age: 11

I have a young brother called Gordon,
Whose appetite really is rotten.
He eats sweets all day long,
To grow big and strong,
But the weight has all gone to his bottom!

Stuart McKelvie
Age: 7

There was a young lady called Rita,
Who was asked to appear on 'Blue Peter'.
Said Val 'Lend a hand,
We can't let her stand,'
Said John 'In that case let us seat 'er.'

Christopher Wood
Age: 13

There was an old man from the moon,
Who thought he'd fly home by balloon,
The balloon it did burst,
The man came off worst,
And landed back home rather soon.

Jim Ferguson
Age: 10

There was an old man from Dover,
Who when he walked always fell over.
When they asked him why,
He went very shy,
And said 'It's my very long pullover.'

Rowena Kerry
Age: 12

In hot weather a farmer named Doyle,
Would wrap himself up in tin foil,
In a cool place he'd store
Himself and he'd snore,
For he feared in the heat he might spoil.

Bruce Smith
Age: 10

There was a young girl from 'Blue Peter',
On her travels was faced with a cheetah,
Though John looked a good meal,
There was no package deal,
'Twas the bite out of Pete that was sweeter.

Joanna Simpson
Age: 13

There was a young man called Pete,
Who was always extremely neat,
His shirts and his ties
Were a sight for sore eyes,
And on colour TV 'twas a treat.

Tessa and Simon Coleman
Ages: 8 and 10

68

There was young cannibal Ned,
Who used to eat onions in bed.
His mother said 'Sonny,
It's not very funny,
Why don't you eat people instead?'

Gillian Nash
Age: 11

There was a young fellow called Noakes,
Who was one of the nicest of blokes,
He chats on for hours
Climbs very high towers,
But never remembers his jokes.

Peter Gibbins
Age: 10

There was a young girl called Pippa,
Who never did wear a slipper,
She lost all her toes,
Because the ground froze,
And had to make do with a flipper.

Philippa Belton
Age: 8

There was a young girl from Crackers,
Who was a wizard at playing the clackers,
The balls flew off,
And got lost in the loft,
So she decided to play the maracas.

Sarah Astell
Age: 10

There was an unusual cat,
That wore a black bowler hat.
He went for a walk,
And began to talk,
What a curious thing was that.

David Harrison
Age: 7

There was a young duckie called Lang,
Who had a very big fang.
He went to a dentist,
Who was an apprentice,
And shot out that fang with a bang!

Bruce Walton
Age: 7

There was a man called Edward Lear
Who wrote limericks like this one here,
But his were much better,
Than the one in this letter,
That's 'cause my brain's a bit queer.

Elizabeth Boon
Age: 11

There was an old spinster from Barry,
Who finally decided to marry.
When questioned why,
She gave the reply,
So the shopping, my husband can carry!

Kathryn Hayward
Age: 13

I have a silly old rhino,
Who ran in and fell on the lino,
So if you now see,
A rhino's bumped knee,
You'll know that the rhino is mine-o.

Stephen Smith
Age: 7

Three brothers from Clacton-On-Sea,
Tuned in to the BBC,
Their favourite treat
Was to see Val, John and Pete,
While eating jam doughnuts for tea.

Dale, Clive and Karl Lockyear
Ages: 9, 8 and 4

There was an old wizard of Wells,
Who made up ridiculous spells,
He magic-ed his beagle,
Into an eagle,
And now on Ben Nevis it dwells.

Nicholas Hartill
Age: 10

There was a young lad called Davy,
Who hated the food in the Navy,
He couldn't have beef,
In case his false teeth
Would drop out and fall in the gravy.

Raymond Coleman
Age: 10 years 11 months

There was a young lady of Leeds,
Who was constantly doing good deeds,
As she bit her young brother,
She said to her mother,
'I'll bind up the wound if it bleeds.'

Christine Tailby
Age: 7

Australia is proud of her 'Kelly',
Brazilians are mad about 'Pele',
But in London we know,
When we're stranded in snow,
Our favourite's 'Blue Peter' on Telly.

Peter Sproxton
Age: 10

There was a TV show called 'Blue Peter',
Which made the limerick the wrong metre,
Had it been called 'Red Fred',
Or even 'Green Ted',
It would have made the rhyming much neater

Janine and Ian Keeble
Ages: 10 and 8

There was a small goldfish named Pinkie,
Who went for a swim in the sinkie,
When out came the plug,
He whispered 'Glug Glug,
I'll be all at sea in a winkie.'

Jeanette Pease
Age: 10

76

A daring young lady from Looe,
Took a journey to far Timbuctoo,
She rode on a yak,
With a hard bumpy back,
And arrived there with skin black and blue.

Sarah Absalom
Age: 6

There was an old man of Berlin,
Whose eyeballs were made out of tin.
Whenever he cried,
They went rusty inside,
And brown tear drops ran down to his chin.

J. L. Honour
Age: 11

There was a Professor called Stock,
Who invented a marvellous lock,
He locked himself in
A very big bin,
And never got over the shock.

Andrew Fuller
Age: 9

There was an old lady called Harriet,
Who bought a marvellous chariot.
But alas she forgot,
That a horse she had not,
So she ended up having to carry it.

Debbie Harrison
Age: 11

There once was a funny old king,
Whose parrot had broken its wing.
'Oh dear' he would cry,
'Poor Polly can't fly,
And how can I fix on a sling?'

Lindsey Paton
Age: 7½

79

There was a young man from Sale,
Who wanted to eat a whale,
He mashed it with ease,
And ate it with cheese,
But just couldn't manage the tail.

Ivor Richards
Age: 9

There once was a man who said 'Cor,
Will nobody answer this door?
I've been knocking all day,
And my hair has turned grey,
And my knuckles are terribly sore.'

Gareth McHale
Age: 10

There was a young lad called Michael,
Who tried to ride a cycle.
He got in a muddle,
Fell into a puddle,
And ran all the way home for a cuddle.

Michael Barnes
Age: 7

There was a young man called Rab,
Who sat on a very large crab,
He shot to the moon,
Landed on a baboon,
Who threw him back down on a slab.

Timothy Paul Newman
Age: 7½

There was a young man who loved Stilton,
Who slept every night with his quilt on,
But the smell from his toes,
Crept up to his nose,
And cured that young man's love for Stilton.

Hilton Lord
Age: 10

There was a young fellow from Crewe,
Who'd been a Royalist since he was two.
When he found grass was green,
He cried 'God save the Queen!'
And painted it red, white and blue.

Clare Simmons
Age: 13

There was a young man called Clark,
Who could score from all over the park,
But in the cup final,
His legs turned to vinyl,
And his shot hit the ref on the mark.

Paul Atkinson
Age: 10

There was a dear tortoise called Terry,
He wandered around on his belly,
One day he went far
And was found by our pa,
Watching our new colour telly.

Jason Wilkes
Age: 7

83

There is a maths teacher called Rundle,
Who ties up his books in a bundle,
It's too heavy he feels,
So he's put it on wheels,
Now Rundle can trundle his bundle!

Amanda Chew
Age: 13

There was an old teacher named Brass
Who was blessed with an unbrainy class,
They slept and they snored
And completely ignored
Theorems like 'Pythagoras'.

Susan Owens
Age: 15

In a tank in my room live two fish,
And they told me that they have one wish,
To be fed twice a day,
On mushrooms and hay,
And have it served up in a dish.

Alan Chatfield
Age: 7

There once was a dinosaur Fred,
Who liked to eat nothing but bread,
But it had not been invented,
So he grew thin and dented,
And soon he was lying there dead.

Rebecca Read
Age: 12

There was a young farmer named Fry,
Who thought his sick pig would die.
So he gave the sick pig,
Some syrup of fig,
Now it's running all round the sty.

Kathleen Jackson
Age: 10

John Noakes was extremely gymnastic,
His suppleness was quite fantastic.
With his legs on his chest,
He could put on his vest,
'Cause his limbs were attached by elastic.

Anne Hurrell
Age: 10

There is a young man called John Noakes,
Who cannot help making 'mistakes',
His 'foons' and his 'sporks'
Get mixed up when he talks,
But he's one of the best among blokes.

Richard Holton
Age: 9

There was an old man called Sam,
Who sailed in a boat to Japan,
It was shaped like a pot,
And if you're not a clot,
You'll see why it's called a 'Sampan'.

Teresa Jenkins
Age: 10

There was a young dog called Dougal
Who wished he'd been born a poodle,
He rushed round and round,
With his nose near the ground,
And ended up more like a noodle.

Alexander J. McCartan
Age: 7

There was a young man with a horse,
A very keen rider, of course,
He tried to jump over
The White Cliffs of Dover,
But couldn't quite muster the force.

Alison Lyne
Age: 9

THE
END

Fiction & Non-Fiction

True Adventures and Picture Histories

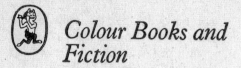

Colour Books and Fiction

COLOUR BOOKS

Great new titles for boys and girls from eight to twelve. Fascinating full-colour pictures on every page. Intriguing, authentic, easy-to-read facts

DINOSAURS Jane Werner Watson
SECRETS OF THE PAST Eva Knox Evans
SCIENCE AND US Bertha Morris Parker
INSIDE THE EARTH
Rose Wyler & Gerald Ames
EXPLORING OTHER WORLDS
Rose Wyler & Gerald Ames
STORMS Paul E. Lehr
SNAKES AND OTHER REPTILES
George S. Fichter
AIRBORNE ANIMALS George S. Fichter

25p each   Fit your pocket – Suit your purse

FICTION
For younger readers

ALBERT AND HENRY
Alison Jezard   20p
ALBERT IN SCOTLAND
Alison Jezard   20p

These and other PICCOLO Books are obtainable from all booksellers and newsagents. If you have any difficulty please send purchase price plus 5p postage to P.O. Box 11, Falmouth, Cornwall.
While every effort is made to keep prices low it is sometimes necessary to increase prices at short notice. PAN Books reserve the right to show new retail prices on covers which may differ from those advertised in the text or elsewhere.